Introduction To Cryptocurrency

Facts, ideas and concepts about digital currencies

By

Austin Winans

Copyright © 2018

All right reserved. No portion of this book may be reproduced, stored in a retrieval system, or transmitted in any form or by any means – electronic, mechanical, recording or otherwise – except for brief quotation in printed reviews without the prior written permission of the publisher or the author.

Table of Contents

INTRODUCTION 4

CHAPTER ONE 7
   WHAT IS CRYPTOCURRENCY? 7

CHAPTER TWO 14
   TYPES OF CRYPTOCURRENCIES 14
      Top ten cryptocurrencies in the world (2018) 15

CHAPTER THREE 23
   CRYPTOCURRENCY WALLETS 23
      Types of cryptocurrency wallets 25
      Examples of cryptocurrency wallets 28

CHAPTER FOUR 31
   A GUIDE TO TRADING CRYPTOCURRENCY 31
      Ways to determine a trade 32
      Tips for trading successfully 33
      Top ten steps for success in cryptocurrency trade 35

CHAPTER FIVE 41
   TOP TRADING WEBSITES 41
      Top trading cryptocurrency exchanges 43

CHAPTER SIX 50
   CRYPTOCURRENCIES AND OUR SOCIETY 50

CONCLUSION 55

Introduction

Innovation drives the world; it is the breath of fresh air we all crave because it comes with a lot of positive changes that make our world better. If there is one concept that will remain all over the world for years to come, it will be innovation that is driven by technology. Cryptocurrencies are a product of such innovative ideas, and they have become a vital part of our society; every investor who is interested in having a dynamic investment portfolio is investing in crypto coins, and this explains why we are embarking on this lesson that focuses on the concept of digital currencies.

This book has a major objective; to teach the reader about the most vital aspects of cryptocurrencies such that after reading, the reader will be able to take strategic steps towards getting the best out of crypto coins. There is a whole lot of information outlined for readers from the first chapter to the last; if you had questions about how cryptocurrencies work and how they can be useful to you, get ready to receive answers.

We will begin with an introduction to cryptocurrency by giving a breakdown of what it means and then a brief history of how it all started. We will proceed to discover the types of crypto coins (do look out for this chapter, it is riveting). Cryptocurrency wallets are a significant part of the cryptocurrency idea as such; we will not be doing a thorough job with this book if we didn't discuss that, would we?

The fact that you are interested in cryptocurrency means you may want to trade or invest, so head over to the section that contains the steps you can take towards purchasing with cryptocurrency. As you learn about how to buy, you might also want to know more about the trading websites that are available to you at this time in the market; there is indeed something for everyone interested in cryptocurrencies.

You are reading a complete guide that contains the most current and relevant information on the subject matter. All you have to do now to get started is to sit back, relax and read on as you join in the digital revolution now known as cryptocurrency. The next section marks the beginning of your journey with this book, and it will be all about gaining understanding into what cryptocurrencies are, their unique features and why they are easily the most talked about tenders in the financial world.

Chapter One

What is cryptocurrency?

An understanding of the concept of cryptocurrency is crucial for us to succeed in this journey and in this chapter, you will learn some of the basic concepts of crypto coins. Cryptocurrencies refer to digital assets that can be used by users across national boundaries. Before the launch of the first crypto coin in 2009, the world had not gained knowledge of the possibility of having and using digital currencies. Today, there is increased awareness and broader acceptance of crypto coins such that it has propelled more crypto innovations.

Bitcoin established itself as a currency that can be used in society in 2010 when someone successfully used 10,000 BTC to purchase two pizzas, and since then the Bitcoin, in particular, has become a leading crypto coin that is used in retail stores online and offline. As at August

2018, the Bitcoin was worth more than $68 million, and this shows the level of acceptance. Aside from the Bitcoin, there are other coins (we will learn more about this in another chapter). These coins all come on the scene with a peculiar feature which shows the dynamic nature of the technology.

There is the fiat currency, which is the money we are all used to and then there is the digital currency which unlike fiat has unique features that make it one of the most sought-after investment option by investors. Cryptocurrencies are globally recognized, they have been analysed as being the fastest means of exchange regarding the use of currencies because it relies on the best form of technology known as cryptography. With fiat currencies, it is sometimes too difficult or complex to complete transactions in record time.

Technology has made everything more comfortable, with social media we can converse with individuals across borders, and it is now the same with money. There are no restrictions and boundaries anymore with international payments. So, with cryptocurrency, you have the assurance of speedy transactions that go beyond your physical location. With cryptocurrencies, transactions are irreversible; this is one of the most viable features of crypto coins that has attracted more users in recent years. Upon confirmation and verification of the transaction, the funds cannot be reversed.

Cryptocurrencies are very secure, if you had doubts about your banking system and worried about the safety of your funds, what you need to do is experience the ease of transacting with crypto coins. As a user, you will not have to rely on banks to facilitate transactions, and this also means that the numerous fees collected by financial houses for international operations can be avoided as well. Crypto transactions are done and completed on the blockchain network which is a decentralized public ledger.

When you trade with cryptocurrencies, you don't have to divulge personal information or give details that can be used to trace a transaction back to you. The feature of anonymity has always made crypto trading and investment appealing to investors; think about it this way, you can send and receive funds without having to input your email address, home address or even reveal your next of kin. Knowing that you can perform transactions within minutes and still keep your identity under wraps is always an appealing factor. With cryptocurrencies, there is only the exchange of wallet addresses between users and just like that, transaction is completed on the most secure technology in the world (the blockchain).

One of the significant reasons cryptocurrencies were developed was to bypass the use of official financial institutions such as banks. Investors buy into the idea of having a decentralized network that doesn't require the use of paperwork or intermediaries who obstruct the flow of transactions. Cryptocurrencies are more than an alternative choice right now all over the world; it started out as an alternative to fiat, and some investors just felt good having multiple streams of investment. As the years go by cryptocurrencies, garner a lot of interest, and this explains why more coins are being added to the market.

Getting more knowledge on how cryptos work will expose you to multiple realities about cryptocurrencies yet you will have to exercise a lot of restraint and caution. When you lose a Bitcoin or any other crypto it is lost forever so aside from getting to know all about cryptos; you also need to become aware of the security steps you can take towards protecting your investment from the vulnerabilities of the system.

While we continue to highlight all the critical and advantageous details of cryptocurrencies, it is also essential that we get to know some of the challenges that come with using this currency. Now the first challenge is the fact that cryptocurrencies are highly volatile. Its volatile nature makes the market unstable, and this instability affects the quality of trading and investment. One of the reasons why cryptos aren't stable is because there is no central authority regulating the market as such prices of coins skyrocket and plummet at any time. If you own shares or stocks with companies, you will agree that the stock market is also an unstable terrain yet the reason the stock market still thrives is that there are regulators in place. The fact that cryptos are volatile doesn't mean you cannot invest or trade; you have to exercise a lot of caution when buying. It is essential that you are informed of the risks associated with a crypto coin; being aware of the risks will help you become better prepared for the future.

This chapter has been an introduction to the concept of cryptocurrency; it is a foundational chapter that helps you get acquainted with the basic concepts and features crypto coins embody. You read through a brief history of the emergence of crypto coins and also got to know about the risks associated with using cryptos. The next section of this book takes the journey up a notch by considering the types of cryptocurrencies available in the market. It promises to be the enlightening and engaging chapter, flip over and enjoy the read!

Chapter Two
Types of cryptocurrencies

Welcome to the section that displays the various kinds of cryptocurrencies available in the market today. The previous part introduced cryptocurrency to you with some essential features and concepts you should know about. Now building on what we know, we are going a step forward by getting to know more about cryptos but this time with more focus on the coins themselves. This chapter will help you become acquainted with the best coins available in 2018, so you can make better trading choices.

To be very detailed, we will take the top ten crypto coins in the world right now; these are the coins that are mostly used by traders and investors because they have proven to have very important market capitalization over the years. Are you ready to read through? Let us begin.

Top ten cryptocurrencies in the world (2018)

1. Bitcoin (BTC)

This is the very first cryptocurrency created in 2009 by a person who uses the pseudonym Satoshi Nakamoto. The Bitcoin is a digital coin that uses a publicly distributed ledger technology called the blockchain. Being the oldest crypto, Bitcoin has the largest number of investors, and it is the easiest coin to purchase because it is adopted by the top wallets and exchanges. BTC has a market capitalization of $163 billion and market share of 36%; it is the most widely accepted coin in the world. Bitcoin has grown regarding market cap; in 2010 1 Bitcoin was traded for less than a Dollar and in 2017, the same Bitcoin $17, 900.

2. Ethereum (Ether)

This is the second most valuable coin that was created in 2015. What Ethereum has is also a blockchain platform for developing decentralized apps and smart contracts, and it is quite popular. If you think about launching an ICO then what you need is the Ether coin, more importantly, the transaction speed of Ethereum is within minutes against the 10 minutes it takes on Bitcoin. This coin has given a 17,000% increase through its $9 performance in January 2017 to its $1389 in January 2018.

3. Ripple (XRP)

This crypto coin is focused on solving problems and is also very proficient in international payment transfers. Released in 2012, Ripple has changed the dynamics of the international money transfer game; it takes up a week to transfer money internationally, but with Ripple, this kind of transfer is done within seconds. Ripple also has the lowest fees per transaction making it one of the most sought-after crypto coins in the world. This crypto coin is currently being used by American Express, and this shows the level of acceptance it has in the market. Ripple has been on the scene for a long time, but it didn't show signs of progress till 2017; now it is the third largest crypto coin with a market cap of $34.12 billion.

4. Bitcoin Cash

This coin was taken from Bitcoin itself; the coin was forked into BCH meaning it was created to solve some problems of Bitcoin especially concerning transaction fees. Bitcoin Cash transactions are faster than Bitcoin due to the increase in block size from 1 MB to 8 Mb. Bitcoin Cash has developed quickly over the years from its inception in 2016; it grew from $500 in July 2017 to $4,000 in December 2017.

5. EOS

This is a current coin that launched in July 2017, and it raised over $700 million in its ICO by January 2018.

Their token price has experienced a significant increase, and it wasn't affected by the market crash that happened in 2018. EOS is already popular even before the launch of its platform; however, you are advised to tread carefully because at the time of this writing the platform hasn't launched, so we don't know how it will turn out despite its huge popularity scale.

6. Cardano (ADA)

This coin was created in September 2017 by Charles Hoskinson who is the co-founder of Ethereum and just like Ethereum; it was created for decentralized apps and smart contracts. There are a lot of technological improvements with Cardano, and these changes are what makes it quite different from Ethereum. This coin boosts of over 257 transactions per second making it more scalable than Ethereum, and it has reached a market cap of $9.35 billion despite being new on the scene.

7. Litecoin (LTC)

Litecoin was built on the Bitcoin blockchain with the aim to make it better. Created in 2011 by Charlie Lee, the coin has done its best to remain relevant seven years after. The Litecoin transaction takes about 2.5 minutes to complete, and this is a massive improvement from the $10 minutes it takes wit Bitcoin. More so, an average Litecoin fee is at $0.179 which is better than Bitcoin's $1.8. with a market cap of $9.64, this coin has experienced growth and isn't about to slow down now.

8. Stellar (XLM)

This coin was created by the founder of Ripple, and it is all about making international payments easier to perform. Stellar is more decentralized, and because it is a non-profit, it becomes a coin that is easy to trust by users. In less than nine months, this coin grew from $0.0039 in April 2017 to $0.85 in January 2018; it is one of the top ten coins because it has continued to grow and get better with time.

9. IOTA

Instead of using blockchain technology, IOTA uses "Tangle," and it is focused on ensuring that transactions are secure, scalable and seamless. Now, this is the most interesting fact; IOTA has zero transaction fees! The technology that backs it up is also quite impressive, making it a unique coin for investors and traders alike.

10. NEO

This is a Chinese crypto coin that was created in 2014, and they just got rebranded in 2017. It is quite similar to Ethereum hence the reason it is referred to as Chinese Ethereum. This network can complete 10,000 transactions in a second unlike Ethereum that completes 15 transactions, and it has the backing of the Chinese government which means it has added advantage in the Chinese and Asian market. In January 2018, this coin reached $162 from $0.16 in January 2017 and had since had an impressive ride.

As a potential trader, it is vital for you to know most of the coins that are available in the market; this is because you will want to invest in as many coins as possible, so you have a dynamic portfolio. If you trade with only Bitcoin, when the market experiences a downturn, you will be significantly affected because all your investments are just with one coin. However, the story is entirely different when you invest with more one currency, if one is concerned, there is every possibility that the other will thrive.

We continued from where we stopped with the previous chapter by considering the types of cryptocurrencies available in the market for you as a crypto trader. There is a list of the top ten cryptocurrencies in the world currently this year, and this list will be handy when you are set to trade on a platform. Before we get to the chapter that highlights how you can sell, we must make a stop at the section on cryptocurrency wallets, after all, we just learned about coins where else are we going to store the coins we are going to buy? The next chapter provides answers to these questions and much more.

Chapter Three
Cryptocurrency wallets

We are still marching on as we take on the concepts of cryptocurrencies piece by piece. We started out by focusing on the features of digital currencies, then moved on to discuss the types of coins available in the market especially the top ten coins in 2018. Now we are ready to discover more, but this time the attention is on the types of wallets you can use as a trader with crypto coins. The objective of this chapter is to enlighten you on some of the most viable purses that will help you on this journey as a trader.

Before we get to the types of wallets, you should know what a crypto wallet means. If you use fiat currency, you will agree that you need to have a bank account where you store your monies until you need them right? Think about cryptocurrency wallets as that bank account, but this time it isn't a fiat account, it is a digital wallet where you can keep your stores till you are ready to trade or invest.

Your wallet is associated with cryptographic keys that are made up of a string of numbers and letters that are generated from a machine. The numbers are used to unlock access to your coins and also create your wallet address which is used to send and receive funds. The keys are so powerful, and they are not to be shared with third parties as such, the platform you decide on for your wallet is significant.

There are multiple types of cryptocurrency wallets, and in this chapter, we will get to know the types of wallets and some examples of these types of wallets as well (as you read, you will grasp the concept). Firstly, we will begin with the types of cryptocurrencies, I like to refer to these as the classes of cryptocurrency wallets because it is from this class, organizations who operate wallet platforms draw their inspiration from.

Types of cryptocurrency wallets

1. Online Wallet

This type of wallet is in the cloud; you can gain access to your coins using such wallets via the internet from any device. The only challenge you have with this wallet is the fact that it is online as such it is exposed to internet hacks and other vices that are prominent with the internet. If you are going to settle for an online wallet, then you need to be sure that you have all security details in place.

2. Mobile Wallet

Mobile wallets are in the form of applications on your mobile phones; this type of wallet needs to be installed on your device, and you can access it anytime and from anywhere. When using a mobile wallet, you have to secure your mobile device at all times because when your device is compromised, then your wallet becomes vulnerable as well.

3. Desktop Wallet

This type of wallet has to be downloaded and then installed on a computer, you gain access via an installation device, and it is one of the safest options regarding wallets that are available. However, just like the mobile wallet, if your computer is hacked or if it gets infected by a virus, there will be trouble with your coins.

4. Paper Wallet

Paper wallets are a physical copy of your public and private keys printed on a piece of paper. The paper has to be stored in a secure location and funds can be sent via the QR code on the paper.

5. Hardware Wallet

This type of wallet is also referred to as a cold wallet because it is the opposite of the online wallet. It is way more reliable than the online wallet, and it requires the use of a USB device where you get to store your keys and perform transactions. Now when you want to use the USB, it has to be connected to a system and used online and disconnected when you are done with your transactions so most of the time you are offline thus keeping your coins safe from online challenges.

What you read above are the classes of cryptocurrency wallets, and they cut across various types such that as a trader, you have a myriad of options to choose from. There are some examples of wallet apps where you can buy, sell and trade with various coins, I will highlight a few as a way of showing you how these wallets work. Please note that there are several of such wallets that cut across the class provided above, what you have below is just a glimpse into some of such wallets.

Examples of cryptocurrency wallets

1. Coinbase

This is one of the leading crypto wallets in the world. Coinbase is a favourite cryptocurrency exchange, so if you have an account with the exchange, you can use the wallet. It is also possible to use the wallet without signing up to Coinbase exchange platform. This wallet uses two-factor authentication support and multi-signature process that ensures extra layers of security for users. It is also very easy to use.

2. Exodus

If you are searching for a desktop wallet to use them, this is what you need. Exodus has got a broad category of crypto coins to select from with an excellent user interface that makes it easy for beginners to navigate through the platform.

3. BRD

This wallet is free and easy to use, you can purchase Bitcoin and carry out transactions from the app within minutes. Although the focus, for now, is on Bitcoin and Ethereum as such users who seek other coins will not be able to take advantage of the platform.

4. Copay

This wallet accepts the only Bitcoin, and it is straightforward to use. It supports the use of multi-signatures and excellent support for users as well.

Cryptocurrency wallets are very important when discussing or planning how to trade with crypto coins. If you do not have wallets, then there is no way you will be able to transact securely with other users. So as a trader, you must be careful with the platform you chose eventually; the platforms must be secure, popular amongst users and known for excellence in service delivery.

Now you know about coins, and you also know where to store your coins, the next concept we will consider is the steps you can take towards trading with cryptocurrencies. We are gradually getting to the main focus of the book, and with all the information you have received, I believe you are ready to learn how you can trade; discover more in the next chapter.

Chapter Four
A guide to trading cryptocurrency

When you put in the work in trading cryptocurrencies, you can be sure of getting the most fulfilling experience because trading with cryptos has the potential of turning little sums of money invested into a neat profit. This chapter is a guide on how you can trade with cryptos such that you can reap the rewards of trading. Now before we go ahead with the manual you should know that the same way there is a high chance of you making the profit, there is also a high chance of you losing money as such, you need to be mindful of how you trade.

Trading cryptocurrencies means buying a coin(s) and selling it to make the profit. The aim of purchasing any asset is to make more money from it when it is sold. With stocks and other assets, prices can be predictable, but this isn't the same with cryptos; prices can change within seconds, minutes and hours making it possible for a trader to make more profit than expected or experience a loss. The question is this "How do I trade wisely?" "what can I do before I trade?" Find the answers below.

Ways to determine a trade

1. Risk factors

Before taking the step to trade with a coin, you should know the risk factors involved and decide if you are going to accept the risks or not.

2. Speculation

Speculations sometimes have elements of truth in them, so before you start trading, you may want to listen to those who have more experience with trading and what they have to say about a coin.

3. Chart analysis

This refers to when traders consider the trends and examine the fluctuations with currencies to know the patterns that they follow. The charts can reveal how prices will change within seconds, minutes or hours.

With the steps above, you know exactly the steps you can take before commencing trading, and it is s essential because if you can get this right, then trading proper will be more comfortable. The next step to take after this is to start trading, and there are some tips you should implement for you to succeed with your trades.

Tips for trading successfully

1. Practice, practice, practice

To be good at trading, you have to practice regularly. Before you decide to trade all the way with as many funds as you've got, you should first practice demo accounts where there are no real losses or risks.

2. Be informed

I cannot stress how important this is enough; you've got to be told by reading books such as this one, listening to the crypto news and getting to know more about what you are getting involved with.

3. Don't chase losses

When you lose, don't go about chasing it and trying to wish it away because losses are a vital part of the process. Accept a loss, learn from it and move on swiftly.

4. Trade with money you can lose

More importantly, ensure that you are trading with money you are comfortable losing. Be prepared for the best experiences, yet you should also expect the worse as such the money you use should not be too important to you at the time.

We are still on the guide to trading successfully with crypto coins, and we have learned two very vital concepts already, they include; how to determine trade and the tips for trading successfully. We will be taking on the next phase of this section, and it is based on the top ten steps you can implement for trading success.

Top ten steps for success in cryptocurrency trade

1. **Learn about the currencies**

You must become informed about the coins themselves, and this demands a lot of reading and learning time. When you know the coins, your choices will no longer be limited, and you will get the best of all you trade with as well.

2. Research before investing

Some traders do not take the time to carry out due diligence on coins before they invest and this leads to huge losses with their currencies. The time you spend on research before investing or trading will help you curtail a lot of errors and mistakes.

3. Learn the basics of trade

There are key areas you must consider when trading and this refers to some of the aspects of trading you must imbibe like signing up to exchange and always checking the crypto space for changes with coins.

4. Sign up for an exchange

This is so crucial because without an exchange you might be unable to trade. Exchanges are the platforms, they are like the marketplaces now, and you need to know what is going on in the market at all times.

5. Learn advanced trading systems

Various types of trading systems and analysis help you predict how cryptos will perform in the market. Get to learn these sophisticated analyses so you can take the right steps at all times.

6. Plan an exit strategy

At the beginning of your trading experience, you should decide exactly when you want to get out. Keep close and watchful eyes over your money and get to know the limit of what you can lose.

7. Listen to crypto news

Cryptos are always evolving, and the best way to keep up with the latest trends and changes in the market is by following the story. Be updated and don't let anything new get to you after it is no longer relevant.; be alert at all times.

8. Get to know about market, limit and stop orders

Market order means selling at the coin's market price; limit orders means setting the rate at which you want to sell; when it hits the limit, your account completes the transaction. Stop orders limit the risk of losses and also guarantees a profit from good price movement. You must become conversant with these terms as a crypto trader.

9. Learn about blockchain

Trading is always high-speed as such if you don't take action immediately, you will be left behind. So, it is vital for you to understand the technology behind cryptocurrencies and that technique is referred to as Blockchain. Knowing all about blockchain and how it works will help you make better choices and help you trade wisely.

10. Trust history

History is always a reliable source when it comes to how we use cryptos. Before you start selling with a coin, get to know the coin's past, its previous market cap, and other essential aspects because history will give insight into how the currency will cope in the market.

Without any shadow of the doubt, you will be able to trade with any coin when you implement all of the ideas and steps shared with you in this chapter. Now it is crucial for you to understand that beginners do not just go ahead and purchase coins without prior information or knowledge on how trading works. As a beginner, you will have to be proactive with these steps.

Trading with cryptos after learning so much about it is a sign of your willingness to take the next step towards getting the best out of all you know. The information you've received will be of no use to you if you are not using it effectively. The next chapter takes you into the world of cryptocurrency websites (also known as exchanges) where the trading and investment happens.

Chapter Five
Top trading websites

Getting to know how to trade with cryptocurrencies isn't enough, you also need to become aware of the various types of sites through which trading takes place because it is only through such platforms, you will be able to trade successfully. We have just learned the steps to selling using Bitcoin, and as exciting as it may have sounded, numerous websites offer the same process.

Why are we concerned about all of these other websites? Well, with cryptocurrency, you do not narrow down your choice of coin, wallet or exchange to just one because of the level of instability. This means that you need to become aware of the options you've got and then chose from the options, the most secure and easy to use platform that helps you carry out successful trades anytime and anywhere in the world.

Aside from looking for regulated exchanges, you also need to search for websites that offer sales of coins you are interested in. For example, if you want to trade with Bitcoin, Altcoin, and Ethereum, and you are signed up to an exchange that doesn't buy with any of the examples above, what do you do? More so, some exchanges do not accept payment in fiat currencies while others do, these aspects must be considered before you go ahead and invest in a particular exchange.

We will analyse some of the best exchanges in the market and the kind of features they've got. There are thousands of transactions out there as such we will not be able to exhaust it all but the few we will take below, are the top exchanges in 2018 that are currently being used by a lot of traders and investors.

Top trading cryptocurrency exchanges

1. eToro

This exchange is one of the world's leading social trading network where new traders can learn from older traders how to position themselves successfully for sale. eToro has got an advanced risk management tool that protects your position as you handle withdrawals, deposits, and transfer of funds. To find out more about this exchange and get signed up visit www.etoro.com

2. Coinbase

Coinbase currently has over 200 million-page views per month because it is one of the most user-friendly exchanges that makes traders happy. It has an attractive interface and is an excellent site for you to get Bitcoins with your debit card. There are over 30,000,000 users signed up to this exchange already, and this site works well with European and American customers. At first, Coinbase started with just Bitcoin; now it takes Bitcoin Cash, Ethereum and Litecoin. Visit www.coinbase.com to sign up and do get ready to trade with ease and with a high sense of security.

3. Binance

This is a China-based exchange that started selling in July 2017, it is new to the exchange market, but it has proven itself to be reliable to users. You have a vast array of coins here including some coins that are rare. Thus, you can experience easy entry and exits. Although it needs time to gain the trust of users, it has started on a very positive note, and it will go on to be better with time. Visit www.binance.com

4. Bittrex

Bittrex has clarified their status by stating that they are compliant with the SEC's ICO rules. It has earned a new flow of users and has become a favourite fast exchange for users to trade with Bitcoin and other crypto coins. There are over 200 trading pairs with high volume coins available for big trades. Bittrex is also trusted by millions of traders, www.bittrex.com is the place to visit now!

5. Localbitcoins

This exchange is known for p2p (Person to person) transactions; this type of deal entails you interacting directly with the person selling to you. There are escrow and dispute resolution on the site, and it is also a great way to meet other traders. Localbitcoins is popular in countries around the globe, and most cases verification isn't required, when you visit the website www.localbitcoins.com

6. Cex.io

This is one of the international bitcoin exchanges that accepts euro, US Dollars, British Pounds, Zcash,

Ethereum, and others. One essential feature you get with the exchange is the transparency with buying and selling. You have the option to buy 100, 200, 500 or 1000 USD worth of Bitcoin, and this is good because it shows the trader how much is to be paid even before the trading happens. It is a modern site, very safe and the exchange accepts bank transfers and credit cards; it is a unique exchange that guarantees results so visit www.cexio.com

7. Kraken

What strikes you about this exchange is the natural verification process. It has the cheapest and fastest trading, depositing and withdrawing times. This exchange works best in Europe and North America; all issues previous users had with the site have been rectified, and by visiting www.kraken.com you will be home to one of the most viable exchanges in the world.

8. GDAX

This exchange is quite refreshing for technical traders, and it offers a high level of liquidity. Deposits are made in USD, and such deposits can be processed with the same speed as withdrawals. GDAX is already optimized to become a severe trading exchange, www.gdax.com is where you should be now as you kickstart your trading activities.

9. Xcoins

Excellent customer service, easy verification, and two-factor authentication are just some of the most peculiar features you are about to discover With Xcoins as soon as you pay the ledger, you get your Bitcoins immediately. They have a peer-to-peer lending system that connects both the lender and the borrower hence, some users of the platform get Bitcoins as a result of secure loans. Check out www.xcoins.com

10. Bitstamp

This exchange is quite known and prominent in Europe, and they have been at the forefront since 2011. You can use your Mastercard or visa to transact, and all transactions are relatively easy to use for beginners. It is sad to note that this exchange isn't available outside of the European Union and United nap. Visit www.bitstamp.net

The list you've got above are just a few of the examples of exchanges you've got in the market, but they are also the top exchanges in the market in 2018. Settling for a good transfer, means you are also getting prepared for successful trades that are not limited by coin type, security or user-interface. Good exchanges combine all of these features, and at the end of the day, the trader is excited about his/her sales and purchases.

The next chapter is all about demystifying the connection between cryptocurrency and society. How has society contributed to making cryptos better? Are cryptos here to stay for good? Can you take cryptos out of society? Head over to the next chapter and enjoy the read.

Chapter Six
Cryptocurrencies and our society

We have been on a fantastic ride since we started this book, so much has been given through the sections and I believe you have learned a lot already. Well, just rounding off the chapter on some of the top trading websites, we will take a break from the technical aspect of cryptocurrencies and talk about the connection between cryptos and society. This chapter's objective is aimed at presenting the facts about cryptocurrency in communities and how it all fits.

Cryptocurrencies are a product of society because the individuals who created them are a part of our community, this means that whatever we do with them, will find meaning in society. Crypto coins were designed to disrupt the pattern that society has currently, did they succeed? Oh yes, they did because, with the advent of cryptocurrencies, man and society can bask in the feel of advanced technology and how it has helped shaped the way we transact.

The connection between cryptocurrency and society begins from the fact that society has embraced cryptocurrency making it one of its payment options for some online and offline shops. There are more shops accepting cryptos for items bought or services rendered. This link between cryptos and society is an indicator that so long there are businesses in society; cryptos will be needed.

Secondly, society has provided a level playing field for cryptos such that there are more users of cryptocurrency now than in time past. Think about it for a minute, why are market caps growing steadily? They are increasing because traders and investors are buying into the idea of having digital coins that replace the stress and delays that come with fiat currencies.

Cryptocurrencies will always be relevant in society, yet some coins will not survive, we mentioned this earlier on in a previous chapter, and it is essential that as you embark on this career as a trader, you get to know that some coins will eventually die out leaving the ones that are stronger. The survival of any currency is dependent on the way society reacts to the coin; some coins die because no one buys them anymore as such their market cap reduces and affects sales.

When talking about the future of cryptocurrencies, one may be tempted to be sceptical because of how volatile they are yet we cannot afford scepticism because, despite the instability, there will be cryptocurrencies in societies in the future. As a trader, your job is to continually figure out ways through which you can continue to make progress with your investments while being mindful of the times and seasons with cryptocurrencies.

If you weren't sure about the way cryptos are connected with society, I believe you are quite sure now because we just read through a chapter that seeks to showcase how both ideas need each other to make it work. Society is the environment where all crypto creations thrive and manifest themselves, if you weren't interested in crypto, I wouldn't be writing, and you wouldn't be reading as well.

This chapter brings us to the end of the book, and I know for sure that it has been the most fantastic ride. The next section contains a message for you that will help give a well-rounded conclusion to this journey; do flip over and enjoy the read.

*Please note that most of the ideas embedded in this chapter are subject to change at any time because the cryptocurrency market isn't a static one.

Conclusion

The world is not going to slow down for anyone anytime soon; there will a lot of changes in the technological space and cryptocurrencies are the fore. Some coins may die out eventually, and some others will forge ahead, whatever happens, the fact that we have had cryptocurrencies exist in the world and use them is a sign that they will be used in the future as well.

What we have achieved with this book is to gain greater insight into the most crucial aspects of cryptocurrency, and I believe you have learned a lot enough to take steps towards trading with cryptos. Let's have a recap of all we read as you get set to sell, invest, learn and grow your cryptos. We started out with an understanding of what cryptocurrency mean, the significant features of digital currencies and a brief history of the creation of digital coins.

The next chapter we considered was about the various types of cryptocurrencies available in the market; please note that not all coins will survive in the future. You have got all of these coins as plausible options for investment but what you need to do with this information is always to update your knowledge about coins, so you are not exposed to unnecessary risks. Cryptocurrency wallets were also discussed because trading will not be possible without wallets.

There is a section on how to trade, and it was quite an extensive chapter as you got to learn steps on how to sell successfully with crypto coins. You got a comprehensive list of all top trading websites and then got an idea into how cryptocurrency works in society. Wow! What an enlightening journey, there is so much more for you to learn and implement but this is a perfect start, what you need to do now is built on all you have gained through constant practice.

Easy to use, fast, secure, globally accepted and absence of third parties are just some of the exciting features that cryptocurrencies embody, you will become a part of a digital culture that is a break from the norm regarding how financial systems work. Yes, there are challenges and issues with the stability of the coins, but this is the peculiar nature of most investments. The vulnerabilities do not put a stop to investing and trading, it only helps you become careful and mindful of how you spend.

Thank you for being such a good sport by getting to the end of this book, when we started, you had an idea of what cryptocurrency is about, but now you have been empowered to do more with what you know now. What do you do as you bring this book to a close? Get set to buy your first crypto coin, sell, invest, buy some more and trade continually; the best way to become good at something is to do it repeatedly. No one became an expert on cryptocurrency by just reading, and they had to add some action to their knowledge. The more they invested, the more they grew, they made mistakes, traded some more and got better with time. You can become an expert, but first, your first coin purchase awaits!

Best Wishes.

www.ingramcontent.com/pod-product-compliance
Lightning Source LLC
Chambersburg PA
CBHW031549210526
45464CB00003B/1215